Photographs and text by Joan V. Lindsay

Third Edition

The Third Edition of "Chicago from the River"® 2010 attempts to expand and update impressions (photos) and rekindle memories of the Chicago River Architecture Cruise.

Published by
Joan V. Lindsay
284 Eaton
Northfield, IL. 60093
email: j.lindsay18@yahoo.com

Copyright Number TX4212637 - 1996 - "CHICAGO from the River"® 2010 Third Edition of "CHICAGO from the River", "Chicago from the River " and the Chicago from the River logo are registered trademarks owned by the Joan V. Lindsay publishing company, all rights reserved.

No part of this publication may be reproduced or transmitted in any form or by any means, electronic or mechanical, including photocopy, recording, or any information storage or retrieval system, without permission in writing from the copyright holder, Joan V. Lindsay.

ISBN 978-1-4507-2145-5

Library of Congress Control Number 2005925254

Distributed by Independent Publishers Group
814 N. Franklin St.
Chicago, IL. 60610
phone: 800-888-4741
www.ipgbook.com

Printed by Unique Active LLC
5500 W. 31st Street
Cicero, IL 60804
www.activegraphics.net

Designed by Vera Shearon-Ball, io design, inc. www.iodesigninc.com

Editorial Consultants - Jane H. Clarke and Suzanne Lindsay Lyhus

Photographs & Illustrations
History-The David R. Phillips Collection (DRPC)
Map of Chicago 1853, page 6, DRPC
1856 Photo, page 6, owned by author
1856 Illustration, page 6, Northwestern University Library Special Collections
    and DRPC
1860s "Crib" or Intake, page 7, Northwestern University Library S.C. and DRPC1860s
Water Tower and Pumping Station, page 7, N.U. Library S.C. and DRPC
Sanitary & Ship Canal 1890s, pages 7 and 42, Metropolitan Water Reclamation District of
    Greater Chicago
Lakefront aerial photos, mid 1920s and mid 1930s, page 12, DRPC
Aerial Photo Outer Drive and "S" Curve mid 1930s, page 7, DRPC
Outer Drive Bridge aerial mid 1930s, page 16, DRPC
Under River Bridges 1920s, page 25, DRPC
Main Branch 1890s, page 38, DRPC
Bridges & Barge mid 1940s, page 50, DRPC
"Ceres" Roman Goddess of Grain 1920s, Inset page 45 John Storrs, sculptor - Ryerson
    and Burnham Libraries, Art Institute of Chicago
Photo taken from Lake Point Tower 2004, page 14, courtesy of Lorry Wolf
Photo of author 2004, page 5 - Sonia and Carlos Sanz

All other photographs by the author

Table of Contents

Introduction	5
Map of the Tour	4–5
Historical Background	6–7
Chicago's Lakefront	8–17
Main Branch	18–25
Fork in the River	26–27
North Branch	28–39
South Branch	40–51
Index	52

CHICAGO from the *River* *Map of the Tour*

Oak

44
45
46 47   Chicago   42
41
40 Erie   Franklin Wells La Salle Clark Dearborn State   Michigan Columbus
39
38   Ohio
                                              Wabash   11
37   Illinois   8
                                                    6   5   4
48 50 Kinzie   24 10 21   7 9
   34   25   28 27 26 22 15 12   13
35 33 51   68   69   70   29   30   23 20
36   71   19 17
   52   54 58   Wacker Drive   14
           55   Lake   18
   31
         56   Randolph
   32   Washington
      53 59
   49   Madison
                   Monroe
                   Adams
            65
         16   Jackson
            64 66 67
                   67b
                   Van Buren
                                              Lake Shore Drive
         Congress Parkway
                   Harrison
         60
         Roosevelt Road & Bridge 61

*
3

Map Legend

1. **Navy Pier**
   1916, Charles S. Frost
   1995; Reconstruction, Benjamin Thompson & Associates
2. **James Jardine Water Filtration Plant**
   1952-1964, C.F. Murphy
3. **Chicago Lock,** 1930s
4. **Ogden Slip**
5. **River East**
   1905-1920, Christian Eckstorm
   1990; Renovation, Booth Hansen Associates
6. **Cityview Condominiums**
   1991, Gelick Foran & Associates
7. **Chicago Tribune Tower**
   1925, Hood & Howells
8. **Medinah Athletic Club**
9. **NBC Tower**
   1989; Skidmore, Owings & Merrill
10. **Trump Tower**
    2009; Adrian Smith, Design Partner Skidmore, Owings & Merrill
11. **Lake Point Tower**
    1968, Schipporeit-Heinrich
12. **The "Hole"**
    foundation work for Chicago Spire
13. **Outer Drive Bridge**
14. **Lakeshore East**
    Master Plan: Skidmore, Owings & Merrill
15. **Riverview Condominums**
    2004, DeStefano and Partners
16. **Willis Tower** (formerly Sears)
    1974; Skidmore, Owings & Merrill
17. **Aqua**
    2009; Jeanne Gang, Studio Gang
18. **Aon** (formerly Standard Oil, Amoco)
    Edward Durell Stone and Perkins & Will, 1973
19. **Swissôtel**
    Harry Weese and Associates, 1989-1990
20. **Michigan Avenue Bridge**
    1920; Bennett, Pihlfeldt and Young
21. **Wrigley Building**
    1921-1924; Graham, Anderson, Probst & White
22. **London Guarantee Building**
    360 North Michigan Ave.
    1923, Alfred S. Alschuler
    2001; Renovation, Lohan Associates
23. **333 North Michigan Ave.**
    1928, Holabird & Root
24. **IBM Tower,**
    1969, Mies van der Rohe
25. **Marina Towers**
    1959-1967, Bertrand Goldberg Associates
26. **75 E. Wacker Dr.**
    (Mather Tower)
    1928, Herbert Hugh Riddle
    1983; Renovation, Harry Weese & Associates
27. **35 E. Wacker Dr.**
    (Jewelers Building)
    1926, Giaver & Dinkelberg
    1980s Renovation, Murphy/Jahn
28. **One East Wacker**
    1962; Shaw, Metz & Associates
29. **Leo Burnett Building**
    35 W. Wacker Dr.
    1989; Kevin Roche, John Dinkeloo & Associates
30. **R.R. Donnelley Center**
    77 W. Wacker Dr.
    1992; Ricardo Bofill, Arquitectura DeStefano and Partners
31. **Lake St. Bridge**
32. **Boeing**
    100 N. Riverside Plaza
    1990, Perkins & Will
33. **Chicago & Northwestern R.R. Bridge,** 1909
34. **Kinzie Street Bridge,** 1909
35. **River Cottages**
    1988; Harry Weese & Associates
36. **Fulton House**
    (North American Cold Storage Warehouse)
    1981, Harry Weese & Associates
37. **River Bank Lofts**
    Wallace Printing Company
    1909, Nimmons & Fellows
38. **600 N. Kingsbury**
    2002, Solomon Cordwell Buenz & Associates
39. **Erie on the Park**
    2002, Lucian LaGrange Architects
40. **Erie Cafe,** 1911
41. **Two River Place**
    2003, Pappageorge/Haymes
42. **John Hancock Tower**
    1969; Skidmore, Owings & Merrill
43. **Kendall College**
    (Converted Warehouse)
44. **Domain Condominiums**
    (Montgomery Ward Warehouse North)
    1905, Richard E. Schmidt
    2002 Conversion; Pappageorge/Haymes
45. **600 W. Chicago Ave.**
    (Montgomery Ward Warehouse South)
    2002 Conversion, Gensler
46. **One River Place**
    (Montgomery Ward Offices)
    1929, Willis McCauley
    2002 Conversion, Fitzgerald Associates
47. **The Montgomery**
    (Montgomery Ward Office Tower)
    1974, Minoru Yamasaki
    2004 Renovation, Papageorge/Hames
48. **Kinzie Park**
    2001, Pappageorge/Haymes
49. **Citicorp Center**
    (North Western Atrium Tower)
    1987, Murphy/Jahn
50. **East Bank Club**
    1980, Gordon Levin & Associates.
51. **Apparel Center&Holiday Inn**
    1977; Skidmore, Owings & Merrill
52. **The Residences at Riverbend**
    2002, DeStefano and Partners
53. **Civic Opera Building**
    1929; Graham, Anderson, Probst & White
54. **333 W. Wacker Drive**
    1983; Kohn Pedersen Fox
55. **191 N. Wacker Drive**
    2002, Kohn Pedersen Fox
56. **123 N. Wacker Drive**
    1988, Perkins & Will
57. **Masonic Temple Building**
    1892 Burnham & Root (not shown)
58. **225 W. Wacker Drive**
    1989, Kohn Pedersen Fox
59. **AT&T Corporate Center**
    1989; Skidmore, Owings & Merrill
60. **River City**
    1984, Bertrand Goldberg Associates
61. **Roosevelt Road and Bridge**
62. **181 W. Madison,** Cesar Pelli
63. **Presidential Towers**
    1980s, Solomon Cordwell Buenz
64. **311 S. Wacker Drive**
    1990, Kohn Pedersen Fox
65. **190 S. LaSalle St.**
    1987; Phillip Johnson, John Burgee
66. **Insurance Exchange Building**
    1912, D. H. Burnham
    1928 Addition; Graham, Anderson, Probst & White
67. **Chicago Board of Trade Building**
    1929; Holabird & Root
67a. 1980 Addition, Murphy/Jahn
68. **Merchandise Mart**
    1929; Graham, Anderson, Probst & White
69. **Helene Curtis Building**
    325 N. Wells St.
    1912, Gustav Hallber
    1982 Renovation; Daniel Coffey & Associates
70. **Reid-Murdoch Center**
    1914, George Nimmons
    2002 Renovation, Daniel Coffey & Associates
71. **Seventeenth Church of Christ, Scientist**
    1968, Harry Weese & Associates

Dedication

Joan V. Lindsay, author, photographer and docent

There would be no book without the City of Chicago and its legendary river...fun to be along for the ride!

I'm most grateful to the thousands of tour-goers with whom I've shared the Chicago River and Lakefront for their enthusiastic responses. It's a privilege to be a docent for *Chicago Line Cruises*; Terry Johnson, Principal.

While most of the images and text from the second edition of *Chicago from the River* are still valid, two new skyscrapers on the Main Branch have dramatically transformed the skyline: Aqua Tower and Trump International Hotel and Tower! These innovative structures are already at home among Chicago's architectural landmarks.

Special thanks to: Vera Shearon-Ball, graphic design; David R. Phillips, Chicago Collection of Historic Photographs; Suzanne Lindsay Lyhus, for writing and editorial contributions; and Doug Lindsay, for constant encouragement.

My husband, Robert Strom, made the third edition possible. I am grateful for his love and support.

Joan V. Lindsay

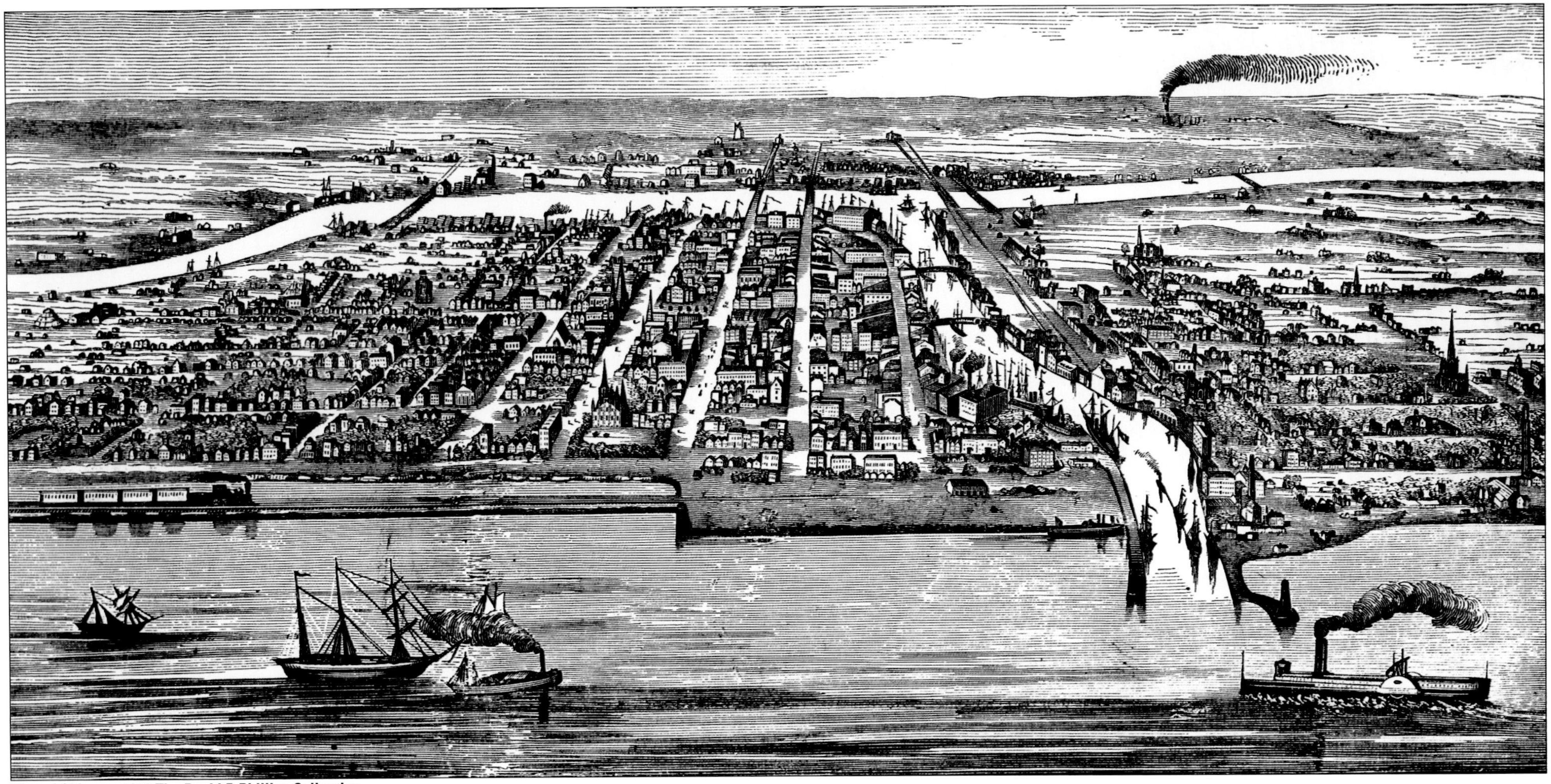

CHICAGO *from the* River

Map of Chicago, 1853 The David R Phillips Collection

A map was drawn up of land for sale in the 1830s. It specified that the lakefront would not be sold, but remain "forever open, clear and free"... a place where Chicagoans could come to refresh their spirits.

In 1852, contrary to the intent of the map, the city gave the Illinois Central Railroad permission to run a trestle up the lakefront in exchange for building breakwaters to protect the business district from the ocean-like effects of the lake. A basin was created between the trestle and Michigan Avenue, which was the shoreline at that time.

In 1871, debris from the Great Chicago Fire was shoved into the basin, expanding "informal landfill" and beginning Chicago's lakefront park.

In this 1856 photograph, a man is standing on the bank of Michigan Avenue. Looking north across the basin formed by the trestle of the railroad, we see grain elevators on the Chicago River.

A more romanticized image of the same scene, this period illustration shows the terminal of the Illinois Central Railroad (left center) at the north end of the basin with grain elevators to its right.

History

By 1890, the lakefront was a sea of railroad tracks, rubbish, and often dead animals. **Montgomery Ward,** wealthy from his invention of the mail order catalog, looked out from his office tower on Michigan Avenue. Sickened by the sight, he called in his lawyer, "This is a damned shame... let's sue the city....[get them to clean up the lakefront for the people of Chicago]." He filed three lawsuits and won all three based on the 1837 map. Ward's courageous acts were the first steps toward the creation of the city's glorious "front yard"!

This aerial photo from the 1930s shows not only the "S" curve but also the "sea of railroad tracks" that Montgomery Ward abhorred! The David R. Phillips Collection

Daniel H. Burnham, Chief of Construction for the *1893 World's Columbian Exposition*, set the stage for the "City Beautiful" movement with the fair's *White City*. Burnham continued the process with his "Plan of Chicago," 1909. The plan included wide streets and boulevards, parks along the lake, as well as in neighborhoods; the transformation of Chicago from an industrial eyesore into "Paris on the Prairie." Progress toward this inspirational goal continues to this day.

Chicago became the fastest growing city in recorded history. With less than a hundred fur traders and Indians in 1830, to more than a million people by 1890...all because the Chicago River connected Lake Michigan and the Great Lakes to the Mississippi Valley and the Gulf of Mexico. Marquette and Joliet really paddled into something in 1673!

At that time, the shoreline ran just about where Michigan Avenue is today. It was wind-swept dunes backed by a foul-smelling swamp that the Indians called "chicagou"; this translated, "stinks like wild onions and garlic." Fortunately, the French established a thriving fur trade in the heart of the continent, so the King of France sent explorers Marquette and Joliet to see if there might be a connection by water between Lake Michigan and the Mississippi. With the help of the Indians, they discovered that the Chicago River not only flowed into the lake, but that it had a south branch. This connected to the Des Plaines River, which flowed southwest toward the Mississippi and on to the Gulf of Mexico – made to order for the French!

The river drained the swamp and flowed into the lake, which had always been the source of Chicago's drinking water. As the population exploded, industry (meat packing, lumber, and others) used the river as a sewer, poisoning the water which flowed into the intakes near the shore. By the 1850s, there was so much disease that the city decided to move the intakes two miles out into the lake *(a)* to get beyond the poisoning effect. The Water Tower and Pumping Station *(b)* were designed by **W.W. Boyington.** All were parts of a water engineering plan by **Ellis Chesbrough** which was developed to provide Chicago with clean drinking water.

These steps improved the situation until 1885 when torrential rains washed sewage beyond the intakes and, eventually, 200,000 people died of cholera and typhoid. Drastic action was needed. Plans were drawn up and digging began of the *Sanitary and Ship Canal (c)* in 1892. The Canal is a twenty-eight mile long, deep ditch in the bed of the south branch, that took eight years to complete. At the time, it was the biggest earth-moving undertaking in human history!

On January 17, 1900, the city blew up the earthen dam holding back the south branch of the river, and very gently the pull of gravity *reversed* the flow of the river away from the lake, and into the new deep trench that led toward the Mississippi. Although this cleaned up Chicago's drinking water like magic, the folks down-river were not so thrilled!

a **Crib, or intake**

b **Water Tower, 1869 and Pumping Station, 1866**

c **Sanitary and Ship Canal**

Lakefront

The Chicago Harbor Light (✱) was moved overland from the coast of Oregon for the World's Columbian Exposition in 1893. Around 1900 the lighthouse was moved to the end of the break-water where it is today. Originally the light was manned, now computer operated. What a view of Chicago!

The photo on the following page takes us from the main branch with Outer Drive Bridge (far left), all the way to the North Avenue Beach (far right), and the **Chicago Lock** (3), middle lower left.

Navy Pier (1) was built as part of a harbor improvement project in 1916, with Charles S. Frost as the architect. The federal government withheld money for the harbor until the city agreed to build a municipal pier. The city took the money and built the world's largest pier which served passenger and freight vessels, plus provided a site for air shows and public amusements.

By the early 1990s, due to severe deterioration, Navy Pier was rebuilt from under the water up. Benjamin Thompson & Associates, with VOA & Associates, were the architects.

The Ferris wheel on the pier is a tribute to the *World's Columbian Exposition of 1893* when the very first Ferris wheel was a heart-stopping attraction - 250 feet in diameter - 100 feet higher than this one! The restored ballroom on the end of the pier, new exposition and amusement spaces, remarkable *Shakespeare Theater*, *Crystal Garden,* plus dazzling views and water access, make Navy Pier the most popular tourist attraction in the city. North of Navy Pier is the **James Jardine Water Filtration Plant** (2), completed in 1964, by C.F. Murphy Associates.

Lakefront

Chicago's Famous Navy Pier

CHICAGO from the River

Reversing the flow of the river in 1900, caused great concern about the effect it might have on the water level in the Great Lakes. By the mid 1930s, public works projects included installing the Chicago Lock to control the amount of water coming in from the lake.

As you can see in the picture, the lock is the only way in from and out to the lake! The triangle-shaped lock gates were made 35 feet deep to accommodate lake cruise ships that once docked on *Wacker Drive*. As the gates open for boats to come in to the lock, a loud speaker announces, *"All boats must 'secure' to the side of the lock"* to avoid bobbing around like "corks in a bathtub"! The gates close behind them before the opposite gates slowly open to the Chicago River.

The lockmaster's horn blows the "all clear" to proceed...

Colonel Roger Gerber of the Army Corps of Engineers shows Peggy Tagliere of the Metropolitan Water Reclamation District the lock and gate repair project.

The Chicago Lock

Lakefront

The water level in the lake varies from six inches to three feet higher than that of the river, so the boats are "lowered" as the gates open to the river.

The reverse process lets boats in from the river to go out into the lake where they "rise," as the gates slowly open to the lake. Ducks love to play in the strong currents as the lake pours in! Views of Navy Pier greatly improve as we head out into the lake toward the Chicago Harbor Light.

The lock is opened on request, free of charge; larger boats go in first. The Chicago Lock operates on the same principle as the Panama Canal locks.

In the late 1990s, the lock gates were dewatered and repaired for the first time since 1959, when the St. Lawrence Seaway opened. The Army Corps of Engineers worked with city engineers to replace the seals on the ends of the gates and to scrape zebra mussels from the enormous gates.

The Chicago Lock during dewatering and repairs in the late 1990s

Navy Pier (very top) with yellow tour boat docked far above the workers below. This view gives perspective of the depth of the locks!

CHICAGO from the River

Ogden Slip *(4)*, is named for William B. Ogden, who came to Chicago from upstate New York in 1833.

His brother-in-law and a friend had come here previously on a "wild west" adventure, got carried away and spent a hundred thousand dollars of the family fortune on swampy real estate on the north side of the river. Ogden decided he'd better come to Chicago to check out this "investment." He got off the boat, landed in mud up to his knees and thought the men had made a dreadful mistake. Ogden put the whole parcel up for auction, sold a third of it, and was amazed when he made his hundred thousand back - plus a big profit! He promptly took the other two thirds off the market, moved to Chicago and was elected the first Mayor in 1837. He and his brother-in-law formed a real estate partnership; **Abraham Lincoln** did the legal work!

Over the years the Ogden family developed the land east of Michigan Avenue. This included Ogden Slip, which was first dug to serve as a lumber yard. Later, it became **Pugh Terminal Warehouse,** and is today **River East** *(5)*.

Ogden slip, mid 1930s; also shown: the Lock and Outer Drive, with its controversial "S" curve, under construction. *The David R. Phillips Collection*

Ogden Slip and lakefront in the 1920s, *before* the installation of the Lock and the Outer Drive. *The David R. Phillips Collection*

The famous *Chicago Architectural River Tour* started here twenty some years ago. Tours still leave from Ogden Slip today.

At the west end of the slip, **Cityview Condominiums'** *(6)* curved towers, frame an elegant view of the **Chicago Tribune Tower** *(7)*. To the Tribune's right, you'll see the **Medinah Athletic Club** *(8)*, complete with *onion-shaped gold dome*.

To the left of the Tribune building, the **NBC Tower** *(9)* incorporates right-angle supports, or contemporary "flying buttresses." They echo those on the crown of the Tribune Tower. The NBC Tower is a textbook example of **Art Deco Revival Style**, emphasizing simple vertical lines, with no historical ornament on the setbacks. Left of NBC, **Trump** *(10)* pushes the skyline to new heights.

Ogden Slip today

CHICAGO from the River

Exiting east from Ogden Slip, is this stunning view of **Lake Point Tower** *(11)*.

In 1938, **Mies van der Rohe** came to Chicago from the Bauhaus Design Academy in Germany to become Dean of Architecture at the *Illinois Institute of Technology.*

In 1968, **George Schipporeit** and **John Heinrich**, former students of Mies, designed Lake Point Tower. It is thought to be derived from a triangle-shaped, glass skyscraper form designed by Mies in 1921.

Mies consistently used *I-beam* mullions as decoration. Rising between the windows, they emphasize the full height of the tower and give rhythm and texture to the curving glass envelope.

Just west of the Outer Drive Bridge is the "Hole" *(12)* — **the foundation for the Chicago Spire, designed by Santiago Calatrava proposed to be a mixed-use building. (Location indicated on following page)**

This perspective from Lake Point Tower showcases the many changes surrounding the **Outer Drive Bridge** *(13)*. On the south side we see **Lakeshore East** *(14)*, the second largest land development in the world - eclipsed only by Canary Wharf in London. The **Riverview Condominiums** *(15)* on the north side, were designed by **DeStefano and Partners**. The **Willis Tower** *(16)*, with its white antennas, indicates the western edge of the loop and gives us a sense of our location from this most eastern point of the city.

Lake Point Tower

Lakefront

View from Lake Point Tower

▲ "Hole" Location for site of Chicago Spire (see inset page 14)

CHICAGO from the River

The dedication of the Outer Drive Bridge by *President Franklin D. Roosevelt* on October 5, 1937, drew thousands of proud Chicagoans. The bridge towers reflect the *Art Deco* influence of that time. Constructed of streamlined Indiana limestone, with no historic decoration, they frame the entrance to the Main Branch of the river.

Amazing changes since the mid 1930s when this photo was taken. The bridge and the Outer Drive are under construction, while the north side of the river, all the way to the Wrigley Building on Michigan Avenue, is filled with warehouses and factories. The David R. Phillips Collection

Outer Drive River Bridge today

CHICAGO *from the* *River*

Main Branch

18

Main Branch

Due west from the *Outer Drive Bridge*, this magnificent panorama shows how two new skyscrapers, **Trump** *(10)* and **Aqua** *(17)*, have transformed the skyline!

Trump International Hotel and Tower commands our attention as we emerge. It majestically rises to 92 stories - now the second tallest building in the United States! Adrian Smith designed its glistening facade of stainless steel and glass which mirrors the landmark buildings and city around it. Trump's soaring silhouette, with setbacks at three levels, reenergizes the skyline.

Aqua displays ample justification for its prestigious, gold medal, **Emporis** award for "Skyscraper of the Year" in 2009. Its fluid exterior gives the impression of water cascading to the ground, reminiscent of the waters of **Lake Michigan** and the rocky outcroppings that line its shores. Jeanne Gang, principal and founder of Studio Gang Architects, is the first woman architect to enjoy this kind of world-class celebrity. Her architectural achievement conveys enormous optimism to all who aspire to the "built environment."

Aqua provides vivid contrast to the Modernist buildings on either side. **Aon Center** *(18)*, originally designed by Edward Durell Stone and Perkins & Will in 1973 for Standard Oil, began as the world's tallest marble-clad building - until one of the marble slabs detached and penetrated a neighboring roof. At great expense, the building was later resurfaced in white granite and remains a tribute to the Modernist style. To the right of Aqua, stands the **Swissôtel** *(19)*, a shimmering glass triangle by Harry Weese & Associates which was completed about 1990.

CHICAGO *from the* *River*

Main Branch

A priceless "Chicago moment" is captured when the yachts come up the river to hail the summer season and the bridges do their "ballet."

The **Michigan Avenue Bridge** (20), often called the "architectural heart of Chicago," was a top priority in **Daniel Burnham's** famous *1909 Plan of Chicago*. The Bridge's opening facilitated the development of North Michigan Avenue, beginning with the **Wrigley Building** (21), one of Chicago's most recognizable landmarks. The Wrigley's castle-like tower (Spanish Renaissance style, in general, and Seville's *Giralda Tower*, in particular) has dazzled visitors and Chicagoans alike since 1921. **Charles Beersman**, talented young designer with **Graham, Anderson, Probst & White**, gets credit for the trapezoid shape that fits the unusual lot. The story is that Wrigley said, "I want it to look like white frosting dripping down a cake." Six shades of white terra cotta (baked clay that's fireproof - very popular in Chicago after the Great Fire of 1871) did the job.

Rising like a phoenix on the site of the former Chicago Sun-Times building is **Trump International Hotel and Tower.** Even as Trump commands our attention with its soaring presence, it reflects the architectural history and context which surround it. A visit to the setback deck on the sixteenth floor affords a superb perspective of our "architectural heart."

Completed in 2009, it was designed by **Adrian Smith** who was at the time Design Partner with **Skidmore, Owings & Merrill. Smith**, currently at **Adrian Smith+Gordon Gill Architecture,** also designed the *Burj Dubai* in the middle-east; now the world's tallest tower.

CHICAGO *from the* River

Looking west beyond the south end of the Michigan Avenue Bridge

This photo gives us a visual history of Chicago's architecture. On the south side of the river, the curved shape of the **London Guarantee Building** *(22)*, built in 1923, is a **Classical Revival** tribute to Greece and Rome. The shape salutes the bridge with a colonnade at the top, complete with tempietto.

In 1928, **333 N. Michigan Ave.** *(23)* brought **Modernism** to Chicago's architecture scene. Eliel Saarinen's Second Prize design in the 1922 Chicago Tribune Tower Competition inspired the simple vertical elegance with gentle setbacks at the top. Quite a contrast to the Tribune Tower *(7)* on the next page; its **Gothic Revival** design won first prize.

Next to Trump is IBM Tower *(24)*, the last building **Mies van der Rohe** designed before he passed away in 1969.

Bertrand Goldberg broke the box with the "Chicago Corncobs." The curving cast-concrete forms of **Marina Towers** *(25)* were Chicago's first "city within a city," a concept Goldberg later repeated on the south branch.

Goldberg, an avid sailor, liked this photo of Marina Towers with masts in the foreground.

The Chicago Tribune Tower was famous long before its appearance in 1925. The *Chicago Tribune Design Competition* in 1922 drew world-wide attention, attracting 264 entries from 23 countries. First Prize went to New York architects, **Raymond M. Hood** and **John Mead Howells**, for their Gothic Revival design.

The crown of flying buttresses at the top recalls the *Butter Tower* of the Cathedral of Rouen, France (ii, below) from the 13th century.

Fragments from famous structures throughout the world are embedded in the base of the Tribune Tower at the request of the Tribune's publisher, *Colonel Robert R. McCormick (1880-1955)*.

(ii) **The Butter Tower of the Cathedral of Rouen, France**

Looking north at the Tribune Tower beyond the Michigan Avenue Bridge

CHICAGO *from the* River

75 E. Wacker Dr. *(26)*, originally the Mather Tower, is Chicago's slenderest skyscraper and was the tallest in the city – for a whole week! **Herbert Riddle** was the architect. A 1983 renovation was executed by **Harry Weese & Associates**. Many years later, terra-cotta "chunks" fell on Wacker Drive! The Drive was closed and re-cladding of the Gothic tower began immediately.

The domed tower to its left is **35 E. Wacker Dr.** *(27)*, originally the Jewelers Building. During the roaring twenties, an internal parking garage gave a feeling of security to the jewelers. Ironically, the decorative pavillion on top housed a "speak easy" which welcomed all manner of unsavory characters! Now a presentation showroom for architect **Helmut Jahn's** office, the full circle view from there is both historic and breathtaking.

In stark contrast to the Jewelers Building is **One East Wacker** *(28)*, a modern column designed in 1962 by **Shaw, Metz & Associates**; later renovated by **Lucian LaGrange & Associates** in 1989.

Irish-born architect **Kevin Roche** made his Chicago debut with the **Leo Burnett Building** *(29)*. Designed to resemble a giant classical column with base, shaft and cornice; the dignified gray-green granite facade is enlivened by stainless steel mullions set into the windows. Roche received a gold medal from the *World Congress of Architects,* who met in Chicago at the time of this building's debut in 1993.

Here the bridges salute the **R. R. Donnelley Center** *(30)*, designed by Spanish architect **Ricardo Bofill** with **James DeStefano** of Chicago. The architects created a triangular pediment atop a glass column shaft, ornamented with flattened columns top to bottom. When the building was dedicated in 1993, the designer from Barcelona quipped, "There's hardly any white marble left in Portugal because we used it all in this lobby."

This haunting photo, taken in the 1920s, seems to look into the soul of the river. David R. Phillips Collection

Main Branch

CHICAGO *from the* River

Looking down the south branch

Heading west, we come to the fork in the river. Looking to our left, we see the **Lake Street Bridge** *(31)* open over the south branch. It is one of the many two-level *bascule* bridges that span the river. Here we see it open to reveal sailboats making their return down-river to storage or warmer climes.

The **Boeing Building** *(32)*, originally *Morton International*, draws our attention. **Ralph Johnson of Perkins & Will** thought it was time for a more "revealing" kind of architecture style from the glass "slipcovers" of the 1980s. In 1990, he showed what was going on *inside* the building on the *outside*. Two columns of offices are separated with a silver stripe of elevator shafts between them. The electrical core is under the clock tower - "what you see is what you get"!

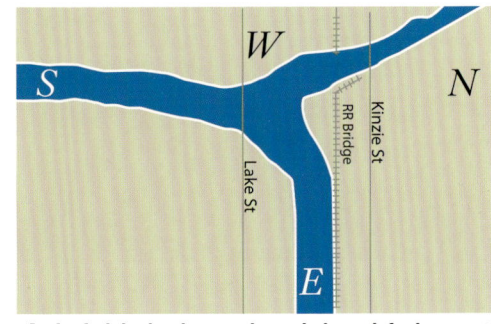

At the fork in the river on the main branch facing west

Fork in the River

Looking north, we see the **Chicago Northwestern RR Bridge** *(33)* and the **Kinzie Street Bridge** *(34)*, both constructed in 1909. The raised black railroad bridge is a perfect example of trunnion bascule technology. "*Bascule*" means "see-saw" in French. The black leaf is counter-balanced by the chunk of concrete that hangs over the river bank. It operates on a trunnion like a giant "teeter-totter"- beautifully balanced and only requiring a motor the size of a Volkswagen engine.

Behind the RR bridge, is the world-famous Kinzie Street bridge. In April of 1992, the city attempted to sink new pilings in front of the yellow bridge house and pierced the ceiling of an old freight tunnel that runs sixty-some miles under the Chicago Loop. The result was the "Chicago Flood." A million people were "walked" down and out of the Loop because the accident left the city with no electricity! Finally the "leak" was discovered and vain attempts to plug the hole by sliding mattresses down the riverbank failed. Repaired at last, the Kinzie Street bridge will most likely be linked to Chicago's underground flood in the city's history.

Directly left of the bridge, the triangle-shaped **River Cottages** *(35)* were designed by **Harry Weese** who also adapted the warehouse into **Fulton House** *(36)* condominiums. The biggest challenge was penetrating three-feet-thick walls to provide windows and balconies. The views from Fulton house justified the effort.

North Branch

⟨ Bridges "saluting" provide the perfect entrance to the North Branch. Both the Chicago Northwestern RR Bridge and the Kinzie Street Bridge, constructed in 1909, are early examples of *trunnion-bascule* technology. This technology brought dependability to crossing the river which was not available with the "swing" bridges it replaced. There are over fifty trunnion-bascule bridges spanning the river - more than any other city in the world. In fact, a prime factor motivating the invention of the "skyscraper" was the limited amount of property in the Loop (the area outlined by the elevated train tracks around the business district).

Chicago's Loop is hemmed-in on three sides by water and on the fourth side by a sea of railroad tracks. By the 1880s, buildable space was scarce south of the river. The only way to expand the business district was "up." Fortunately in 1885, **William LeBaron Jenney** put the finishing touches on the steel frame and the first "skyscraper," the *Home Insurance Building*, appeared. Once proven, tall buildings became the norm. Chicago was a thriving manufacturing and transportation center, and was desperate for office space!

⌄ **The River Bank Lofts** *(37)* were the result of an amazing conversion in 1996. The warehouse, originally designed in 1909 by **Nimmons & Fellows** (house-architects for Sears Roebuck), has had many lives. First it functioned as a railway terminal and warehouse, and later housed the Wallace Printing Company. Now this appealing loft building is an example of the trend that artists started many years ago. Hoping to find inexpensive loft space for studios, galleries and apartments in old warehouses; artists began the process of gentrification in areas like River North.

CHICAGO *from the* *River*

The circular "corner" of **600 N. Kingsbury** *(38)* designed by **Solomon Cordwell Buenz & Associates** begins a remarkable stretch of development between Grand and Chicago Avenues.

The white tower in the center, **Erie on the Park** *(39)* was called *"Little John"* in a review by architecture critic, *Blair Kamin*. He compared its "structure" to the *"cross-bracing of Big John"* Hancock on Michigan Avenue. Talented French architect **Lucien LaGrange** designed Erie on the Park.

To the left, at the end of Erie Street, is the low-scale **Erie Cafe** *(40)*. Now a famous Chicago steak house, it was originally built in 1911 as a meat packing warehouse (rumored to have an *Al Capone* connection!). In the distance, towering above the Erie Cafe is **Two River Place** *(41)*.

John Hancock *(42)* towers on North Michigan Avenue in this picture first published in the first edition of *"Chicago from the River,"* in 1995.

What a different view today with "Little John" and other new towers in the foreground!

CHICAGO *from the River*

Up ahead on the right is *Goose Island*, named for flocks of geese brought by the nineteenth-century Irish immigrants who settled there. **Kendall College** *(43)*, occupying another converted warehouse, is the newest resident. Under the bridge, barges filled with concrete mix remind us of the river's industrial past.

This is where the boat turns around...

Goose Island, ahead and right

The former *Montgomery Ward Corporate Center* displays three styles of architecture. The angle-shaped, **Prairie Style** warehouse (farthest left) with continuous horizontal lines, was designed in 1905 by **Richard E. Schmidt** who contoured the building to the shape of the river. In the 2002 conversion, **Pappageorge/Haymes** converted the north segment of the angle into **Domain Condominiums** *(44)*. In 2002, the southern segment of the angle, **600 W. Chicago Ave.** *(45)*, became offices in a renovation by Gensler.

The Spirit of Progress Through Commerce (46a), a sculpture symbolizing pre-depression optimism, appears atop the stepped pyramid. St. Louis architect, **Willis McCauley**, designed this **Art Deco Style** office building for Wards in 1928. Balconies were retrofitted in the 2002 conversion to condos by **Fitzgerald Associates**. The residential reuse is now known as **One River Place** *(46)*.

Architect **Minoru Yamasaki** designed a newer office tower (top center) for the Montgomery Ward Corporation in 1974. Yamasaki modified the **International Modern Style** with marble corners - no corner office windows for Ward's executives! Yamasaki was better known as the architect of the *World Trade Center* in New York.

In 2004 the tower became the **Montgomery** *(47)*, a condo conversion by Pappageorge/ Haymes.

Left to right, Domain Condominiums, 600 W. Chicago, The Montgomery, One River Place

(46a) Stepped pyramid and "The Spirit of Progress Through Commerce"

CHICAGO from the River

View looking south toward Wolf Point in 1995

In 1995, coming down the North Branch was a different picture. A barge was moored where Kinzie Park is today.

The silver-blue **Citicorp Center** *(49)*, originally *the Northwestern Atrium* building designed by **Helmut Jahn**, was clearly visible then.

Today, the Citicorp Center peeks above the town houses of **Kinzie Park** *(48)*.

Across the river, the upscale health and athletic club, the **East Bank Club** *(50)*, was a huge selling point for the Kinzie Park development.

Beyond the East Bank Club, the **Apparel Mart** and **Holiday Inn** *(51)*, anchor historic *Wolf Point*. The mart also houses the *Chicago Sun-Times*.

The **Riverbend** *(52)* condominium tower stands guard at the "fork" in the river.

North Branch

View looking south toward Wolf Point today

CHICAGO *from the* River

◁ This view is the most popular "photo-op" on the tour. The Willis Tower rules the sky with the throne shape of the **Civic Opera Building** *(53)* posing in front. *Samuel Insull,* developer of the Civic Opera Building, supposedly said that he wanted the back of his throne to face New York because Chicago was going to have a *better* opera theater. Architects **Graham, Anderson, Probst & White** obliged the tycoon with this throne in 1929.

To it's right, Boeing, with its "highest clock tower in the world" appears before us again.

We are heading toward the Lake Street ▷ Bridge and the South Branch of the river.

On the left, **333 W. Wacker Dr.** *(54)* was voted Chicago's favorite building in a Chicago Tribune "competition." Designed by New York based **Kohn Pedersen Fox** in 1983, its curving shape beautifully mirrors the bend in the river. **191 N. Wacker Dr.** *(55)* was designed with elegant simplicity by the same firm twenty years later.

Set back to its right is **123 N. Wacker Dr.** *(56)*, a 1988 **Perkins and Will** design. The pyramid cap echoes the pyramid on top of the Civic Opera Building. The Tut exhibit of archeological finds at the Field Museum in the 1980s refocused attention on Egyptian architecture.

North Branch

Looking south toward Lake Street and the South Branch

CHICAGO *from the* River

Main Branch, 1890

North Branch

In this 1890s photograph of the river, "swing bridges" are shown. They swiveled on the piers in the middle of the river, clearly showing why the "Loop" did not expand north, but went "up" instead.

In 1892 **Burnham & Root** designed the **Masonic Temple Building** *(57)*. It remained the "tallest building in the world" for over twenty years! The rooftop gables inspired Phillip Johnson's design of 190 S. LaSalle Street *(pages 44–45)*.

Fast forward a hundred years or so...

It is obvious from both views that the curve in the river presents a formidable challenge. The area had been a triangular-shaped parking lot for many years before **William Pedersen,** partner of the New York firm **Kohn Pedersen Fox,** came up with the spectacular solution you see here, 333 W. Wacker Dr. in 1983. Pedersen gave a **Post-Modern Style** treatment to Chicago's long-established tradition of *"tripartite"* or three part design: base, shaft and clearly defined top.

The graceful, green glass "shaft" bends to the curve in the river and enhances the elegantly reconstructed *Wacker Drive*. Constantly changing light and conditions play off the mirrored surface to the delight of spectators. People who responded to the Chicago Tribune's challenge, *"Vote for your favorite skyscraper,"* gave twice as many votes to 333 W. Wacker Dr. as they gave to any other building!

The award winning design resulted in many more commissions including "next door," **225 W. Wacker Dr.** *(58)*. In 1989, Pedersen wanted 225 to *"complement,* not *compete,"* with his masterpiece. It fits into the context of the beige *"wall"* on the south side of the river. Again he uses "tripartite" design with a base, shaft and decorative towers.

A friend of Pedersen's came on my tour and said the "bridge" between the towers of 225 W. Wacker Drive (left center) was the architect's tribute to the bridges over the river.

We cruise down the South Branch of the Chicago River, with the Civic Opera building on the left and Boeing on the right. Sailboats head down the river signaling the end of the season, but commanding an encore in the *"Ballet of Bridges"*!

A giant leap from the river brings us to this aerial view looking south, with bridges "at ease" on the far right. 123 N. Wacker Dr.*(56)* points "up" toward the Willis Tower*(16)*. Architect **Bruce Graham** worked with genius, structural engineer **Fazlur Khan** (both of **Skidmore, Owings & Merrill**) on the 110 story tower, at that time *Sears Tower*. **Khan**, who came from Bangladesh to study with **Mies van der Rhoe** at IIT, devised the *"bundled-tube"* technology used: he took nine square towers, three on a side, and *"bundled them together"* for stability. All nine rise to the 50th floor where two terminate; two more towers stop at 66; three terminate at 90; and two rise to 110 stories - which made the Sears Tower the "tallest building in the world" for twenty some years. Renamed Willis Tower, it is still Chicago's tallest.

To the left of Willis Tower, the **AT&T Corporate Center***(59)* makes its appearance with pinnacles atop. AT&T is architect **Adrian Smith's** interpretation of a 1920s setback office tower. **Smith**, who was then a design partner at **Skidmore, Owings & Merrill**, acknowledged being influenced by *Eliel Saarinen's* second prize design of the Art Deco setback tower for the Chicago Tribune Competition of 1922.

Bridges "at ease" over the South Branch

CHICAGO *from the River*

⌃ Before turning around, we look south to **River City** *(60)*. In the mid-1980s, Bertrand Goldberg designed another *"city within a city."* This one is quite different from his first, **Marina City,** built in the mid-1960s. River City's curves are wider, and a serpentine interior *"street"* called **River Road** gives residents an *"inside streetscape"* as well as outside views. Designers say these condos are easier to decorate than the pie-shaped ones in Marina City. Year-round "mooring" is available in the marina under River City - but heading south toward the Gulf of Mexico for the winter has appeal! The **Roosevelt Road bridge** *(61)* is south in the distance.

In 1892, it was very near River City's location that the earthen dam was built to divert the flow of the South Branch west to an auxiliary channel. The trench you see in the bed of the river (photo right) was twenty-eight miles long and deep enough that gravity would pull the flow away from the lake into the deep trench toward the Mississippi. According to the newspaper account, when city "officials" blew up the earthen dam, the "straws" they had earlier floated on the river slowly reversed direction. Sanitary engineers were both surprised and delighted to see this proof of their success.

South Branch

Looking north over the south branch, another "sea" of railroad tracks hugs the river bank. Roosevelt Road and Bridge span them both in the foreground. A guidebook published at the turn-of-the-century called Chicago, *"The Railroad Hub of the Universe."* Sitting on the other bank (right), is River City.

Willis Tower dominates the skyline with 311 S. Wacker just in front of it and AT&T*(59)* to the east. To the right of AT&T, we see a setback tower by **Cesar Pelli** from Argentina, **181 W. Madison** *(62)*. Other well-known structures to his credit include the *Petronis Towers* (Kuala Lumpur, Malaysia) and the *World Financial Center* (New York City). The next page shows these from the river – a close-up view. On the left of our aerial photo here, four towers stand like sentinels on the edge of the west loop. **Presidential Towers** *(63)* were designed by **Solomon Cordwell Buenz**. The development sought to ease Chicago's housing shortage in the 1980s.

View from South Branch-Roosevelt Road and Bridge in foreground

CHICAGO *from the* River

With **River City** *(60)* on our right, the South Loop's variety of architecture unfolds. The pink granite tower, **311 S. Wacker Dr.** *(64)*, tries hard to compete with the city's tallest behind it. An irreverent architectural historian calls them *"Chicago's Dynamic Duo."* Architects **Kohn Pedersen Fox** even crowned the tower with cylinders that, when brightly lit at night, look like a white castle on the skyline! Its debut in 1990 proved difficult for the developers, as it was the end of the real estate *"boom"*; it took almost ten years to rent the space.

The array of styles continues, beginning with **190 S. LaSalle St.** *(65)* designed by **Phillip Johnson** in 1985 at the height of the building boom. Fortunate timing helped it fare better financially than 311 S. Wacker and others built a few years later. **Johnson's** gabled roofline resembles the Masonic Temple Building of 1892 by **Burnham and Root**. This is a fine example of architects *"connecting to the past,"* and giving Chicago's architecture historical context.

Masonic Temple

The white terra-cotta clad rectangle with classical columns marching around the top is the **Insurance Exchange Building** *(66)*. Designed by **Daniel Burnham** in 1912, the addition in 1928 was by **Graham, Anderson, Probst & White**. Burnham loved the **Classical Revival** style - Louis Sullivan said it set architecture back fifty years!

The Chicago Board of Trade *(67)* exhibits the simple **Art Deco** vertical styling with *"setbacks."* In accordance with the building code *Ordinance of 1923*, tall buildings had to incorporate "setbacks" to prevent streets from becoming dark canyons.

The pyramid-shaped top has a thirty-five foot sculpture of *"Ceres,"* Roman Goddess of Grain and Agriculture *(67a)* by Chicago artist **John Storrs**. Trees partly obscure **Helmut Jahn's** 1980 addition *(67b)* with a pyramid roof that echoes the one on the Board of Trade. **Jahn** capped his pyramid with a *"stylized trading pit"* that looks somewhat like a hood ornament!

South Branch

Chicago's South Loop 67a, Closeup of "Ceres" by John H. Storrs, 1928 which tops the Chicago Board of Trade building © *Courtesy The Art Institute of Chicago – all rights reserved*

CHICAGO *from the* River

Returning north, we are again greeted by Boeing. All the buildings on the west side of the river were built on the *"air rights"* over the railroads by sinking support columns between the tracks. However, no support column could be sunk at the Boeing building's southwest corner because of a railroad switch yard below. **Ralph Johnson,** architectural engineer with **Perkins & Will,** came up with the ingenious solution to cantilever the bridge-like structure out from the main tower of the building. Johnson's suspended structure made a nice architectural metaphor for the bridges over the river – wonderfully illustrated in these photographs!

CHICAGO from the River

Willis Tower (formerly Sears Tower)

◁ **This unique perspective of Willis Tower from the river illustrates Fazlur Khan's bundled-tube technology. Clear observation ledges project from the 103rd floor.**

Ahead we see the **Merchandise Mart** *(68)* and its stunning reflection in the curving glass of 333 W. Wacker across the river. It is the largest commercial building in the world - completed just in time for the Depression in 1929!

Marshall Field developed the Mart to house wholesale suppliers but would have to sell it to *Joseph Kennedy* for a third of its building cost, about twelve million dollars! Some years later, the Kennedy Family spent a fortune to clean the facade, blackened by decades of coal burning engines. They "cleaned up" financially when they sold it for an enormous profit! The pyramid forms on the towers and the continuous vertical lines suggest the **Art Deco** design favored by the architects in the late 1920s.

Beyond the Mart, **325 N. Wells St.** *(69)* began as the Chase & Sanborn Tea & Coffee warehouse. **Larry Booth** received a gold medal from the American Institute of Architecture for *"adaptive reuse"* when he converted the warehouse into a corporate headquarters for Helene Curtis. The green glass board room on top looks more like a yacht club.

The **Reid-Murdoch Center** *(70)*, with a backdrop of towers on the main branch, was designed in 1912 by **George Nimmons,** as a food storage warehouse. The clock tower was practical at the time because few people had wrist watches. After years as a traffic court building for the City of Chicago, the warehouse was renovated into an upscale office building.

Looking east on the Main Branch: Merchandise Mart, 325 N. Wells, Reid Murdoch Center

CHICAGO from the *River*

Main Branch

A picture is certainly worth a thousand words when it comes to illustrating the river as a commercial artery supplying the city's heart with life-blood.

Early skyscrapers – the Wrigley Building *(21)* and the Jewelers Building *(27)* were landmarks of the office tower boom of the 1920s.

This photo could have been taken any time between the early 1930s to the mid 1950s. During the period of the Great Depression and the Second World War, hardly any new construction took place; the cars suggest the late 1940s.

Industrial use of space is evident with warehouses, railroads, low use of real estate on both sides of the river - signs of the times.

Today, looking east, the main branch appears to terminate at **Harry Weese's Seventeenth Church of Christ, Scientist** *(71)*. With towers at attention lining the river; bridges respectfully give their final *"salute."*

Index

123 N. Wacker Dr. 5, 36, 41
    See Perkins & Will, Christian Eckstrom
1893 World's Columbian Exposition 7, 8
190 S. LaSalle St. 5, 39
191 N. Wacker Dr. 5, 36
    See Kohn Pedersen Fox
225 W. Wacker Dr. 5, 39
    See Kohn Pedersen Fox
311 S. Wacker Dr. 5, 43, 45
    See Kohn Pedersen Fox
325 N. Wells St. (Helene Curtis Bldg.) 5, 49, 51
333 N. Michigan Ave. 5, 23
    See Holabird & Root
333 W. Wacker Dr. 5, 37, 39, 49
    See Kohn Pedersen Fox
35 E. Wacker Dr. (Jewelers Building) 5, 25
600 N. Kingsbury 5, 31
600 W. Chicago Ave. 5, 36
75 E. Wacker Dr 5, 25

A
Adrian Smith 21
Apparel Mart and Holiday Inn 5, 38
AT&T Corporate Center 5, 44, 46
Aon, 5, 19
Aqua 5, 19

B
Benjamin Thompson & Associates 5, 10
Boeing Building 5, 28, 48
Bruce Graham 5, 41
Burnham & Root 5, 39

C
C.F. Murphy Associates. 5, 1
Charles Beersman 5, 21
Charles S. Frost 5, 10
Chicago & Northwestern R.R. Bridge 5, 29
Chicago Board of Trade Building 5, 45, 47
Chicago Harbor Light 5,
Chicago Lock 5, 8, 10, 11
Chicago Sanitary District 20
Chicago Sun-Times 5, 21, 35
Chicago Tribune Tower 5, 13, 22, 23
Chicago's Loop 31
Citicorp Center 5, 35 (Northwestern Atrium Tower)

Cityview Condominiums 5, 12
Civic Opera Building 37, 41
    Colonel Robert R. McCormick "Crib" or Water Intake 5, 7

D
Daniel Coffey & Associates. 7
Daniel H. Burnham 5, 7, 45
DeStefano and Partners 5, 15, 25
Dirk Lohan 7
Domain (Montgomery Ward Whse) 5, 33, 35
Durell Stone

E
East Bank Club 5, 34
Ellis Chesbrough 5, 7
Erie Cafe 5, 31
Erie on the Park 5, 31

F
Fazlur Khan 41,
Fitzgerald Associates. 7, 33
Flood of April 1992, 29
Fork in the Main Branch 5, 27, 28, 37
Fulton House 5, 29

G
Gensler 7, 33
George Nimmons 7, 49
George Schipporeit 5, 14
Graham, Anderson, Probst & White 5, 21, 37, 45,

H
Harry Weese 5, 7, 19, 25, 29, 51
Helmut Jahn 25, 35, 47
Herbert Riddle 25
Holabird & Root 5, 7
Home Insurance Building 29
Howells & Hood 5

I
IBM Tower 5, 22
IIT 41

Insurance Exchange Building 5, 45

J
James Jardine Water Filtration Plant 5, 11
Jewelers Building 5, 25
John Hancock Tower 5, 31
John Mead Howells 23

K
Kendall College 5, 32
Kinzie Park 5, 35, 36
Kinzie Street Bridge 5, 27, 28, 29
Kohn Pedersen Fox. 5, 37, 39, 42

L
Lake Point Tower 5, 14
Lakeshore East 5, 14
Larry Booth 49
Leo Burnett Building 5, 25
Lohan Associates 5
London Guarantee Building 5, 22

M
Masonic Temple 39, 45
Marina Towers 5, 22
Marquette and Joliet 7
Mather Tower 5, 25
Merchandise Mart 5, 49, 51
Metropolitan Water Reclamation District of Greater Chicago 11
Michigan Avenue Bridge 5, 21, 24, 25
Mies van der Rohe 5, 15, 23 41,
Minoru Yamasaki 5, 33
Montgomery Ward 5, 7, 14, 33
Murphy/Jahn 5, 38

N
Navy Pier 5, 8, 10, 11
NBC Tower 5, 12
North Avenue Beach 8

O
Ogden Slip 5, 10, 12, 14
One East Wacker 5, 26
One River Place 5, 33
Outer Drive Bridge 5, 15, 16, 17, 19

P
Pappageorge/Haymes 5, 33
Perkins & Will 5, 19, 28, 48
Plan of Chicago, 1909 6, 21

R
R. R. Donnelley Center,. 5, 25
Raymond M. Hood 23
Reid Murdoch Center 5, 51
Richard E. Schmidt 33
River Bank Lofts 5, 29
River City 5, 43, 44, 45
River Cottages 5, 29
River East 5, 12
Riverbend Condominiums 5, 35
Riverview Condominiums 5, 17
Roosevelt Road 5, 43, 44, 45
Roosevelt Road Bridge 44

S
Sanitary & Ship Canal 5, 7, 9, 44
Schipporeit-Heinrich 5, 14
Sears 5, 29, 41, 50
    See Willis Tower
Seventeenth Church of Christ, Scientist 5, 51
Shaw, Metz & Associates. 5, 25
Skidmore, Owings & Merrill 5, 21, 41
Swissôtel 5, 19

T
Trump Tower 5, 19, 21, 23
Trunnion-bascule bridges 29
Two Prudential Plaza 5, 19
Two River Place 5, 31

V
VOA & Associates. 5, 8

W
W.W. Boyington 7
Water Tower 5, 7
William Le Baron Jenney 5, 29
Willis Tower 5, 36, 37, 41, 43, 44, 48